I0821195

Angora Goats

by Julie Murray

Abdo Kids Jumbo is an Imprint of Abdo Kids
abdobooks.com

abdobooks.com

Published by Abdo Kids, a division of ABDO, P.O. Box 398166, Minneapolis, Minnesota 55439.

Abdo Kids Jumbo™ is a trademark and logo of Abdo Kids.

Printed in the United States of America, North Mankato, Minnesota.

052025

092025

Photo Credits: Adobe Stock, Alamy, Getty Images, Minden Pictures, Shutterstock

Production Contributors: Teddy Borth, Jennie Forsberg, Grace Hansen
Design Contributors: Candice Keimig, Pakou Moua

Library of Congress Control Number: 2024947600

Publisher's Cataloging-in-Publication Data

Names: Murray, Julie, author.

Title: Angora goats / by Julie Murray

Description: Minneapolis, Minnesota : Abdo Kids, 2026 | Series: Fancy farm animals | Includes online resources and index.

Identifiers: ISBN 9798384905226 (lib. bdg.) | ISBN 9798384905929 (ebook) | ISBN 9798384906278 (Read-to-me ebook)

Subjects: LCSH: Angora goat--Juvenile literature. | Goats--Juvenile literature. | Farm animals--Juvenile literature. | Livestock--Juvenile literature. | Domestic animals--Juvenile literature.

Classification: DDC 636.3--dc23

Table of Contents

Angora Goats

Angora goats are known for their long locks of **mohair**. They are gentle and friendly. This makes them the perfect fancy farm animal.

Angoras are a Turkish breed of **domesticated** goat. They were **bred** in **Asia Minor** more than 4,500 years ago. There are very few left in the wild today. Most live on farms around the world.

Europe
Asia Minor
Asia
Turkey
Africa
N
W
E
S

Angora goats are social animals. They need to live in a herd. Only a certain number of goats can live in an area. This is so each goat gets plenty of food.

Angora goats communicate through a crying sound called a bleat. The volume and **pitch** of the bleat can mean different things. The goats also use **body language** and scent to communicate with one another.

Body

Angora goats are smaller than other kinds of goats. Males stand about 4 feet (1.2 m) tall and weigh around 200 pounds (90.7 kg). Females are smaller.

Angora goats are covered in **mohair**. They have horns on their head. The horns of male Angora goats are long and curled.

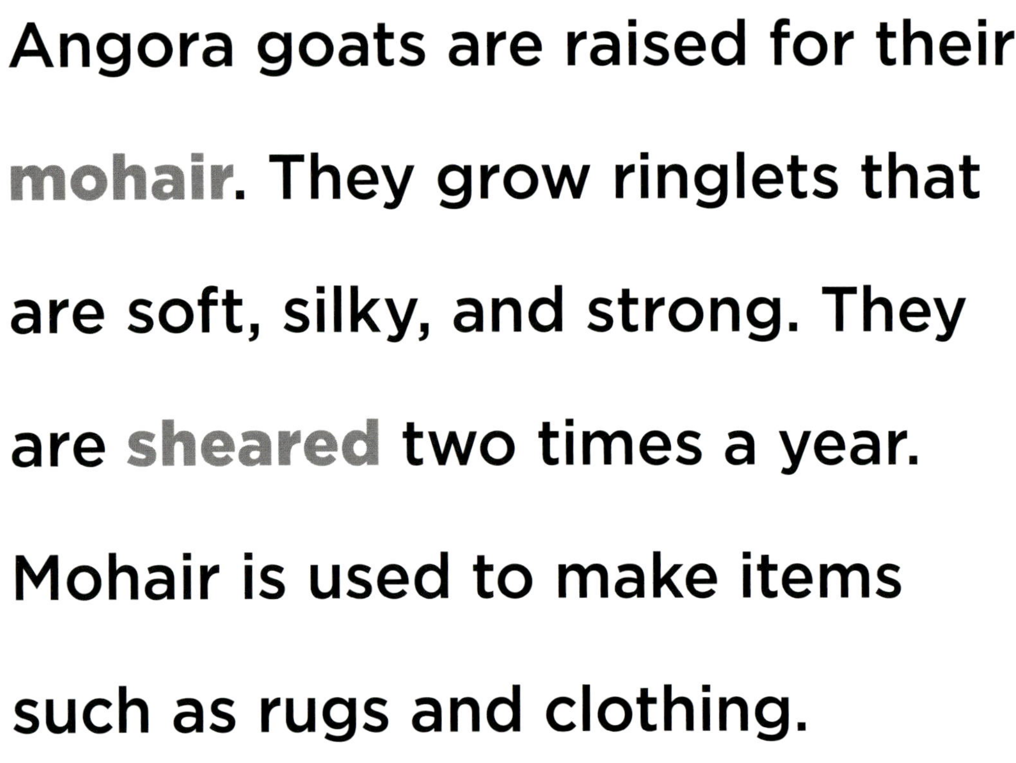

Angora goats are raised for their **mohair**. They grow ringlets that are soft, silky, and strong. They are **sheared** two times a year. Mohair is used to make items such as rugs and clothing.

Diet

Angora goats are **grazing** animals. They eat woody plants, hay, grass, and leaves. They eat about 3 to 6 pounds (1.4-2.7 kg) of food each day.

Baby Angora Goats

Female Angora goats give birth to one to three babies at a time. Baby goats are called kids. They are 7 pounds (3.2 kg) at birth. They drink their mother's milk for four months.

More Facts

- Most Angora goats have white **mohair**. The goats can also be black, brown, or gray in color.

- The mohair of Angora goats grows 4 to 6 inches long (10-15 cm) before each **shearing**. Adults can grow up to 15 pounds (6.8 kg) of mohair each year!

- Angora goats are named after an area in Turkey historically called Angora. Today it is known as Ankara.

Glossary

Asia Minor – a large peninsula in West Asia on which most of Turkey is located.

body language – movements or posture used as a means of communication.

bred – developed over time for a certain purpose.

domesticated – made useful to humans and living near them rather than in the wild.

grazing – feeding on growing grass.

mohair – the long, soft, silky hair or fleece of the Angora goat.

pitch – the high or low quality of a sound or musical note.

shear – to trim the fleece or hair from something.

Index

Visit **abdokids.com** to access crafts, games, videos, and more!

Use Abdo Kids code

FAK5226

or scan this QR code!